The Stress Management Book

Expert Strategies for Dealing With Stress for Men, Women, Teens & Kids

By Brian Shawn

TABLE OF CONTENTS

Disclaimer Notice

This book was written as a guide and for information, educational and entertainment purposes only. No warranties of any kind are expressed or implied.

Readers acknowledge that the author is not engaging in the rendering of legal, financial, medical or professional advice, and the information in this book is not meant to take the place of any professional advice. If advice is needed in any of these fields, you are advised to seek the services of a professional.

While the author has attempted to make the information in this book as accurate as possible, no guarantee is given as to the accuracy or currency of any individual item. Laws and procedures related to business, health and well-being are constantly changing.

Therefore, in no event shall the author of this book be liable for any special, indirect, or consequential damages or any damages whatsoever in connection with the use of the information herein provided.

DEDICATION

**This book is dedicated to my Father
Ulester Mahoney Sr.**

ACKNOWLEDGMENTS

I WOULD LIKE TO ACKNOWLEDGE ALL THE HARD WORK OF THE MEN AND WOMEN OF THE UNITED STATES MILITARY, WHO RISK THEIR LIVES ON A DAILY BASIS, TO MAKE THE WORLD A SAFER PLACE.

Introduction

INTRODUCTION

Think about this simple story about a jar, when problems in your life feel like they are very difficult to tolerate, and when 24 hours in a day are simply not enough.

A professor stood in front of his philosophy class with a few things in his hands. When the class started, he picked up an empty mayonnaise jar and continued to fill it with small balls without saying anything.

He then questioned whether the container was full? A student replied, yes, it was.

After that, the professor took a new package of small pebbles and added them into the pot. He gently shook the pot.

The pebbles rolled between the large balls and filled the open space. He asked the same question, is the jar full? A student replied yes again.

He then took out a sand package and started adding sand to the jar. What about the jar now? He asked! Is it full? A student replied, yes, it is! He took out a water bottle and started adding water to the jar. The water has filled all the space. Look, said the professor, this jar represents your life.

The large balls represent all important things in your life like family, friends, career, health, etc. The pebble represents your job, sand and water represents all other things smaller things that can fill your life up.

INTRODUCTION

If you add sand or water first, you will not find a place for anything else. Same goes for life.

If you think excessively about small things that you can't control, you will have no time for your family. You need to pay attention to things that are most important in your life, to reduce stress.

You may believe that there is nothing you can do to reduce your life stress. Bills will continue to pile up, there will never be enough hours in the day to do any of your unlimited tasks, and your work or family responsibilities will remain demanding.

Millions of people are subjected to extreme levels of stress on a daily basis. Stress is becoming important than ever before in our constantly hectic world.

Consequently, more people are looking for the right stress books that can help them in dealing with stress and other negative physical consequences. So if you are facing this problem and want to get rid of it, then this book is for you.

Constant stress is often caused by self-imposed and crippling standards. This book will guide you about how the mind's natural restlessness can trigger tension and anxiety, as well as share strategies for living a more relaxed or healthy life.

INTRODUCTION

Exercise, diet, music, and meditation are all tools that can be used to help with everyday stress and the mental health issues that come with it. Each chapter in the book will focus on finding a solution for stress-related issues.

This book will provide you sound tips about how to relax and reframe the emotions that are causing the constant anxiety.
The universe may not improve after you read this book; however, your responses to it and your priorities in life will likely change.

In the first chapter, you will read about stress and its basic overview, like what its causes are, and signs and how to manage it. In the second chapter, unique mental solutions are given to cope with stress. You will read about several strategies that will be helpful in managing stress.

In the third chapter, you will read about several physical solutions to stress problems like making time for fun, starting some exercise, listening to music, etc.

In the fourth chapter, some healthy diet solutions are given to assist you. The fifth chapter has important strategies regarding stress management at the workplace, and the sixth chapter will show you some benefits that stress can bring to our life. Yes benefits.

INTRODUCTION

I'm a professional motivational speaker and best-selling author and have studied, researched and spoken a great deal on solutions to stress. After my years of research, I have written this book and have uncovered many real solutions to stress, that don't rely on medication.

This book has easy-to-follow instructions and a style that I hope makes you feel as if I'm speaking directly to your situation. I have some interesting stories to highlight the book's main points and solutions.

I have added easy to use solutions to help readers cope with tension and their overly busy lives in a meaningful way. This inspirational book is the handy tool you've been looking for to help you live a more mindful and peaceful life.

Methods in this book have been tested over time and proven to work. If you work it. If you want meaningful change and like a systematic approach to stress management you will find this book inspiring.

Having a good plan of action, and creating a habit of using the plan on a daily basis, is the key to reducing , managing and even eliminating the feeling of stress in your life.

Let's get started!

Chapter 1:
All about Stress
Management

ALL ABOUT STRESS MANAGEMENT

Once I read a story that really mesmerized me and helped me in a difficult time.

"The carpenter I employed to assist me in rebuilding an old farmhouse had just completed his first day on the job. He lost an hour of work due to a flat tire, his electric saw broke down, and now his old truck wouldn't run.

He sat in silence as I took him home. He called me in to see the family when I arrived. He stopped momentarily at a small tree as we headed toward the front entrance, it looked like he was using his hands to do something to the brances of a tree.

He quickly change after opening the door. He embraced his two small children and kissed his wife, whose face was adorned in smiles.

He then led me back to my car. When I reached my car, I inquired about what I had seen him do earlier. He said, "Oh, that's my worry tree." "I know I can't help but worry at work, but worries have no place in my home with my wife and kids. But every night when I get to my home, I just hang them up on the tree. Then I pick them up again in the morning." "Funny thing is, when I go out in the morning to pick them up, there aren't almost as many as I recall hanging up the night before," he said with a grin. He made me speechless but also taught me a very valuable lesson, agree?

ALL ABOUT STRESS MANAGEMENT

Let's talk about stress

Stress is everywhere around us and stays with us wherever we go. It is a kind of normal physical and emotional response to different life events. We all struggle and fight with stress at some point in our lives. Stress can be triggered by anything, including daily tasks like work and family to major life events like a new illness, battle, or the loss of a loved one. We all handle tension in various ways. Many factors, including heredities, early life experiences, lifestyle, and social and economic conditions, all influence our ability to cope with it.

When we are stressed, our bodies develop stress hormones, which stimulate our immune system and initiate a fight or flight response. This enables one to react rapidly in risky circumstances.

Your body's stress responses assist you in adapting to new circumstances. Stress can be beneficial in that it keeps us conscious, motivated, and prepared to prevent any harmful risk. A stress response, for example, can help your body function harder and stay awake longer if you have an important test coming up.

However, excessive tension may have damaging consequences. As stressors persist without relief or intervals of recovery, it becomes a challenge. If you constantly feel fatigued and tired, it's time to take steps to restore your nervous system's health.

ALL ABOUT STRESS MANAGEMENT

Learning to understand the signs and effects of chronic stress and taking measures to manage it will help you protect yourself and change how you think and behave.

Define stress

When we talk about defining stress, people have a lot of different thoughts about it. There has never been one globally accepted definition of stress. As a result, it's impossible to measure stress if there's no harmony about what constitutes stress.

Widely accepted definition of stress:

One definition of stress is that "physical, mental or emotional tension is called stress."

Another popular definition:

"A disorder or sensation that occurs when a person believes that demands outweigh the individual's ability to organize personal and social resources."

Medical or biological context

Stress is a kind of physical, behavioral, or emotional factor that induces bodily or mental tension in a medical or biological sense.

- It may be internal (from your inner or social situations) or external (from the environment, psychological, or social situations).

ALL ABOUT STRESS MANAGEMENT

- Stresses may be caused by (illness or from a medical procedure).

- The "fight or flight" reaction, a dynamic reaction of neurologic processes, may be activated by any type of stress.

3-stage process; Hans Selye GAS model
Hans Selye (1907–1982) was a very famous Hungarian endocrinologist who was the first to explain biological stress scientifically.

General Adaptation syndrome, the three-stage GAS phase, explains the biochemical changes that occur in the body when it is stressed.

Our Body Response to stress

The General Stress Syndrome is made up of three important sections.

- The warning stage, which is known as the first stage

- The resistance stage, which is known as the second stage.

- The third stage is called a state of fatigue.

ALL ABOUT STRESS MANAGEMENT

First Stage: The alarm stage

The first stage, known as the alarm stage, describes the symptoms that the body exhibits when stressed. The "fight-or-flight" reflex, which is a physiological response to stress, will be your first reaction.

Fight-or-flight response

An angry dog runs out into your street as you're out on a morning run and starts growling and barking at you.

Your coat rack seemed to be a human standing right next to you in the split second before you switched on the lights in your empty home.

All these situations will trigger your sympathetic nervous system, which controls your body's normal fight or flight reflex. This is your body's response to threats, and it was created to aid you in surviving traumatic and life-threatening circumstances.

The release of hormones that support your body to either stand and deal with a challenge or flee to safety triggers the fight-or-flight reaction.

The body's sympathetic nervous system is triggered by the rapid release of hormones in response to stress. The sympathetic nervous system (SNS) stimulates the adrenal glands, causing catecholamine to be released (including adrenaline and noradrenaline).

ALL ABOUT STRESS MANAGEMENT

The blood pressure of the body, heart rate, and breathing rate all rise as a result of this sequence of events. After the danger has passed, the body takes 20 to 60 minutes to return to its previous state. How can our body react during the Fight-or-flight response?

The following physical signs will signify a fight-or-flight response:

Heart rate and blood pressure might be increased

This specifies that you're breathing more rapidly, which aids in the delivery of nutrients and oxygen to the main muscle of the body.

Flushed skin or Pale

Have you ever noticed when your blood supply is redirected, you feel cool or notice that your hands and feet are cold and sweaty. When blood and hormones flow across the body, your face will also become red-faced.

Sometimes don't feel pain

It's not very uncommon to just feel your pain after you've recovered to safety and had time to feel if your sympathetic nervous system has faced any collusion. This is one of the reasons that people injured in traffic crashes usually don't feel pain immediately.

ALL ABOUT STRESS MANAGEMENT

Dilation of the pupils

The body naturally trains itself to be conscious of its surroundings in times of any risk through dilation of the pupils, which lets more light into the eyes, and therefore you have a clearer perception of the surroundings.

Tense or trembling

Since stress hormones circulate across your body, you can feel nervous, as if your muscles are going to twitch.

Bladder

In a highly unpleasant or risky environment, it's not unusual to lose control of the bladder or bowels.

One way to deal with certain conditions is to understand the body's innate fight-or-flight reaction. When you realize that your body is getting tense, you will begin to look for ways to relax and calm down. Psychologists may help patients discover new ways to cope with their innate stress response by learning more about the fight-or-flight response.

Second stage: Resistance

The body continues to heal itself after the initial trauma of a traumatic incident and the fight-or-flight reaction. It produces less cortisol, which causes the pulse rate and blood pressure to return to normal.

ALL ABOUT STRESS MANAGEMENT

And if the body is recovering, it still remains on high alert for a bit. Once you resolve depression and the situation is no longer a problem, the body will start to heal until your hormone levels, heart rate, and blood pressure return to pre-stress levels.

Any tense conditions can last for months or even years. If you don't try to deal with the tension and keep your body on high alert, it will finally adapt and learn to cope with a higher degree of stress. In order to deal with stress, the body undergoes changes that you may not fully understand.

The stress hormone is still being produced in your body, and your blood pressure is still high. You may believe you're handling stress well, but your body's physical reaction says another story. The fatigue stage will occur if the resistance stage is maintained for an extended amount of time without delays to counter the effects of stress.

The following are signs that you're in the resistance stage:

- Irritability
- Obstruction
- Inability to concentrate

Third Stage: Exhaustion

This stage is caused by long-term or persistent stress. Long-term stress will lessen your physical, emotional, and mental energy to the point that your body no longer has the ability to fight with it.

ALL ABOUT STRESS MANAGEMENT

You may be about to give up or believe that life is quite miserable.

Here are some red flags that show you are stressed:

- Fatigue
- Burnout
- Anxiety
- Nervousness
- Insufficiency in coping with pressures

This stage's physical effects can disrupt the immune system and place you at risk for some stress-related illnesses.

Types of stress

There are three main types of stress, according to the American Psychological Association (APA):

- Acute stress
- Episodic stress on a regular basis
- Long-term depression

Each of these three forms of stress has its own set of features, symptoms, time span, and treatment options. We will discuss the fourth type of stress, positive or healthy stress, in later chapters.

Each of these three forms of stress can appear as a single, repetitive, complex, or persistent occurrence; stress control can be difficult.

ALL ABOUT STRESS MANAGEMENT

A person's environment, lifestyle, and psychiatric history cause different levels of medical procedures, management, and therapeutic treatment modalities.

Acute stress

Acute stress normally occurs temporarily. It's the most common form of stress. Reactive thought may cause acute stress. Negative emotions predominate when thinking about current circumstances or activities, as well as potential situations, events, or requests.

For example, if you have recently been in an argument, you might be experiencing acute stress as a result of negative feelings due to the argument. Alternatively, you might be experiencing acute stress as a result of a looming job deadline; this, too, is thought-induced stress. When the stress is caused by thought as soon as it is removed, the stress may disappear as well.

Note: Anyone can be diagnosed with Acute Stress Disorder (ASD) if the stress follows DSM-5 guidelines.

DSM: Diagnostic and Statistical Manual of Mental Disorders

Common signs and symptoms of the acute disorder: Here are some common symptoms of the acute disorder.

ALL ABOUT STRESS MANAGEMENT

Short term Emotional distress: Anger or irritability, anxiety, and depression are also common symptoms. Short term Muscular distress: Tension, jaw pain, back pain, headaches, neck pain, and other physical stresses may result in strained tendons and muscles.

Short term hyper arousal: High blood pressure, a fast heartbeat, a fast pulse, sweating palms, heart palpitations, dizziness, migraine headaches, cold hands or feet, shortness of breath, sleep issues, and chest pain are all symptoms of hypertension.

Other Short term signs: heartburn, acid stomach, diarrhea, and constipation, and all symptoms of stomach, gut, and bowel problems.

Occasionally, mild acute stress does not usually result in mental health issues. However, if it occurs again and again, it can cause serious health problems. This is referred to as episodic acute stress, and it is discussed further below.

Causes of Acute Stress Disorder ASD
A person's ASD may be caused by a number of stressful circumstances, such as:

- Witnessing a close relation death
- Serious accident
- Experience war
- Rape or other forms of sexual assault
- A bodily assault
- Kidnapping or being held captive
- Terrorist threats
- Natural calamities

ALL ABOUT STRESS MANAGEMENT

Episodic acute stress

Sometimes individuals experience acute stress on a regular basis; they are said to be having episodic acute stress. This style is common in people who are short-tempered, irritable, and nervous. They frequently have a negative attitude or are too concerned about everything. They adopt stress as a normal part of life and find it impossible to change their habits.

Individuals who experience extreme tension on a regular basis often live in a state of uncertainty and crisis. They are either rushing or under pressure. They take on a lot of tasks and find it difficult to remain organized with the burden of loads. These people are constantly in a state of extreme stress.

Main personalities

There are mainly two major personality types that experience this stress:

Type A personality

People with "Type A" personality traits are more likely to experience stress than others. Many Type A people are time-conscious, ambitious, and impatient, which can lead to tension in relationships, work, and other areas of life. For the Type A personality, these personality characteristics trigger regular episodes of acute stress.

ALL ABOUT STRESS MANAGEMENT

Anxious personality

People who always remain worried about different things experience episodic acute stress. These people find tragedy everywhere and predict disaster in every situation. For them, the universe is a risky, unrewarding, punishing environment where something terrible is always going to happen. They may always remain agitated and nervous, but they are more distressed and upset than angry or threatening. Their minds are constantly packed with "What if..." statements that have negative consequences.

Common signs and symptoms of episodic acute stress:

The most common signs and symptoms are the same, like acute stress, but there is chronic trauma and pain due to frequent arousal or prolonged hyperarousal.

Emotional signs: Some emotional signs include a tense look, hot-tempered, anxiety and depression, irritability or frustration, impatience, etc.

Cognitive signs: Some cognitive signs include lack of focus or concentration, slow processing speed, difficulty acquiring new skills and consolidating and retrieving new learning memories, and constant mental exhaustion.

ALL ABOUT STRESS MANAGEMENT

Muscular problems: Some muscular problems that people can face include tension, headaches, and back pain, jaw pain, pulled muscles, tendons, and ligament issues.

Stomach related issues: Irritable bowel disease, gut, bowel complaints, heartburn, acid stomach, flatulence, diarrhea, constipation (IBS).

Immune System: Some immune system symptoms include Colds/flu, allergies, asthma, and other immune-suppressing diseases.

More serious issues: If we talk about some serious symptoms, it includes shortness of breath, insomnia, chest pain, and cardiac attack, and all symptoms of high blood pressure.

Resistant to change

Treating episodic acute stress requires intense care on several occasions, which usually necessitates clinical assistance, which can take several months.

Most people's lifestyle and personality traits are so entrenched and habitual that they don't see something wrong about the way they live their lives. It's normal for these people to blame their troubles on other people or incidents outside of their control.

ALL ABOUT STRESS MANAGEMENT

They often regard their lifestyle habits, relational patterns, and ways of perceiving the environment as necessary or central components of their personalities, and therefore are unable to pursue skilled therapeutic support.

Chronic stress

Chronic stress is a type of anxiety that occurs on a daily basis. If not well managed, this form of stress will leave you feeling exhausted and even lead to stress. This is how the body can experience sudden loss if the stress reflex is chronically triggered, and the body is not taken back to a relaxed state until the next wave of stress hits.

Chronic tension, on the other hand, is dangerous as well. This is the kind of persistent tension that wears people down year after year. Chronic stress causes devastation for people's bodies, brains, and life.

When a person cannot find a way out of a bad situation, they develop chronic stress. It's the strain of never-ending demands and strains for what seems like infinity. When a person loses faith, he or she stops looking for answers.

Childhood trauma plays a vital role

Sometimes chronic stress is the result of stressful early childhood events that become internalized and remain debilitating and present for the rest of one's life.

ALL ABOUT STRESS MANAGEMENT

Early childhood experiences have an important influence on personality, often culminating in core value structures that are formed as a result of the individual's constant stress (e.g., the earth is a threatening place, you have to be perfect at all times). Recovery involves active self-examination and specialist counseling support as deep-seated convictions and views need to be reformulated. The good news is that psychiatric therapy is very successful.

Some sort of numbness

Desensitization is the result of repeated exposure to stress for a long period of time. The depressed person may feel overwhelmed to the point that they no longer feel stressed. They can, however, experience the excitement and exhilaration of acute stress while ignoring chronic stress because acute stress is a new occurrence for them.

Worst case scenario

Since acute stress is new, people are acutely conscious of it. Unfortunately, an individual may become so used to the feeling of chronic stress that they become uncomfortable when they are not in the stressful setting. There have been many occasions when I was so stressed out at work that I took a break.

ALL ABOUT STRESS MANAGEMENT

Common signs and symptoms of chronic stress:

The most dangerous kind of stress is chronic stress. Chronic stress, if left unchecked for a long time, may have a serious and sometimes permanent negative impact on your physical and mental well-being. Chronic stress is characterized by the same set of signs and symptoms as episodic acute stress. Chronic stress disturbs almost all of the body's systems.

Here are some important symptoms.

- It can weaken your immune system.
- It can disrupt your digestive and reproductive systems
- It can increase your risk of heart disease and stroke.
- It can increase the aging process
- It has the ability to rewire your brain, making you more susceptible to fear, depression, and other mental health issues.
- Sometimes it causes physical and emotional breakdown that can result in suicide, murder, paranoia, heart attacks, and strokes.

You need immediate help

If you always feel depressed, nervous, overwhelmed, panicked, or stressed out, you need to visit a clinical psychologist who can teach you how to better handle stress. He or she may assist you in identifying scenarios, feelings, and habits that cause discomfort and anxiety in your life.

ALL ABOUT STRESS MANAGEMENT

Developing an action plan to treat you would be part of your treatment. Your well-being is influenced by your surroundings, as well as your body, mind, feelings, and emotions.

Common Causes of stress

Stressors are some specific situations and pressures that trigger stress. We normally associate stressors with the negative, such as a demanding work schedule or bad relationship. Anything that places heavy stresses on you, on the other hand, can cause stress in life. Good activities such as getting married, maintaining a home, going to work, or getting a promotion falls into this category.

External causes do not, however, cause stress. Internal or self-generated stress occurs when you obsessively think over something that could or may not happen or when you have negative, depressive thoughts about life.

Anything that stresses you out does not mean it will bother others as well; in fact, they might love it. While some of us are afraid of performing in front of an audience or giving a speech, others thrive in it. When job demands increase, one person thrives under pressure and performs better in the face of a tight deadline, while another may feel stressed. Although you may enjoy assisting with the treatment of your aging parents, your siblings may find the responsibilities of caregiving to be exhausting and frustrating.

ALL ABOUT STRESS MANAGEMENT

Here's a short review of each of the six major stressors:

- Environmental tension
- Social stress
- Organizational stress
- Physical tension
- Psychological tension
- Stress caused by significant incidents

Environmental stress

Environmental stress will be the first cause of stress, pressure, and anger in your life. This form of stress is about the facets of your life and surroundings that make you feel stressed. Living next to a loud, busy street, for example, can cause you to experience stress symptoms and effects.

Social stress

Social stress is a big cause of stress. This refers to the anxiety that comes with a meeting, socializing, and connecting with other people. It circles around social relationships. Sometimes social encounters and relationships become very difficult and stressful in your life. Others may be pleasurable and beneficial forms of social stress and contact.

ALL ABOUT STRESS MANAGEMENT

Organizational stress

All of us are engaged with and often worked in an organization. This may result in workplace stress.

Some phycologists think this issue comes under the area of environmental or social stress.

It often involves the demands and pressures placed upon you by the company, business, or group for which you work.

Physical stress

Physical stress is the fourth cause of stress. This has to do with how the body reacts to adverse conditions and how you react to them. It's mostly addressed in terms of physical discomfort and the physical stress effects you're experiencing. Take a moment to recall a time when you were afraid, anxious, or trembling. Now think of any of the physical responses to the unpleasant situation. Your body's reactions to stress are part of your physiological reaction to stress.

Psychological stress

Psychological stress is the fifth kind of stress, and it includes the strength of the subconscious in how you think, rationalize, and make sense of your stress, annoyances, and worries. It's all about how your brain, psyche, and mind process tension in your life. It's also known as emotional stress or mental stress, and it's characterized by strong thoughts and emotions.

ALL ABOUT STRESS MANAGEMENT

Significant events stress

Serious accidents and major events in your life are the sixth and final cause of tension. Significant events stress is another name for it. Now, not all stress is negative, and you can experience good stress as a result of major events in your life. High school graduation, a wedding, or winning a professional championship are also examples of this. There are, however, major incidents that cause negative tension. These are often referred to as life's vital accidents. This may include a single major occurrence such as a fatal injury, a physical or sexual assault, and so on. Such occasions elicit a great deal of fear and tension.

Stress statistics by cause

Money, employment, and family commitments are some of the most basic stressors that never change. However, we saw many new stressors in 2020, including the COVID-19 pandemic, a riotous political situation, and more.

- About eight out of ten Americans say the coronavirus (COVID-19) has made them anxious (American Psychological Association, 2020)
- Seventy-seven percent of people in the United States say they are concerned about the country's political situation, up from 66 percent in 2019. (American Psychological Association, 2020)

ALL ABOUT STRESS MANAGEMENT

- In 2020, 63 percent of people in the United States said the economy is a major cause of stress, up from 46 percent in 2019. (American Psychological Association, 2020)

According to a 2017 survey, the leading sources of stress in the United States were:

- Financial resources (64 %)
- Jobs (60 %)
- The state of the economy (49 %)
- Duties of family (47 %)
- Personal health problems (46 %)

How to cope with stress?

You put your complete health at risk if you live under high levels of stress. Stress, without a doubt, has a negative impact on both your mental and physical health. It makes it difficult to think clearly, act efficiently, and enjoy life. It can seem that there is nothing you can do to relieve stress.

Effective stress control allows you to free yourself from the control that stress has on your life, allowing you to be happier, stronger, and more prosperous. The main aim is to live a happy life, with time for jobs, friends, rest, and fun—as well as the stamina to keep going when things get tough.

ALL ABOUT STRESS MANAGEMENT

What is stress management?

Have you ever noticed how a small laugh can help to lighten your load? Maybe you've been in a situation similar to one of these.

Your day is exhausting, so you coach yourself to take a step back, gather your thoughts, and make a list of what needs to be done– prioritizing what is most important. Has your to-do list ever made you see that your day is much more controllable than you think? You may go for a walk with a friend every morning before going to work.

This week seems to be far too hectic and exhausting to have a small break. However, instead of skipping it, you opt to go for a walk. Afterward, you find that it was good for you mentally, psychologically, and emotionally and that as you sit down for the workday, you feel more capable of tackling your to-do list.

Stress management

Stress management requires making lifestyle changes while you are constantly stressed, avoiding stress by self-care and relaxing, and lessening your reaction to difficult situations as they arise. However, stress control is difficult. That's why it's important to try new things to see what works best for you.

ALL ABOUT STRESS MANAGEMENT

Changes are stressful

Change can be very difficult because it forces one to learn and adapt. Too many changes in a short amount of time will give the impression that we are losing control of events. This mindset leads to poor self-esteem and can also lead to anxiety or depression.

When a person's capacity to respond to change is overcome by so much change, physical illnesses may grow or worsen.

You will take control of your health and reduce the effects stress has on your life if you realize the toll it has on you and how to fight it.

It's important to remember that not all stress is negative before moving on to stress control strategies. People all over the world would be more able to manage the negative effects of the stress phenomenon if they better understand it.

The following chapters will give you a variety of strategies that you can use to effectively manage your stress.

People are destroyed for lack of knowledge.

So get excited! And let's get started discovering all the many ways we can manage and defeat the stress challenges in our life.

Chapter 2:

Mental Health Stress Management Techniques

STRESS MANAGEMENT TECHNIQUES

As we all know that it is impossible to remove all stressors; therefore, it is very important to develop strategies for dealing with stress. Knowing the symptoms and stages of stress will assist you in taking the necessary measures to relieve your discomfort and reduce the chances of any serious complications.

What triggers you?

Identifying the causes of stress in your life is the first step in the stress management process. This isn't as easy as it seems. It's very difficult to ignore your own stress-inducing emotions and habits when your real causes of stress aren't always apparent. You may be aware that you are increasingly concerned about meeting job deadlines. However, it's possible that deadline tension is caused by procrastination rather than the real work demands.

You need to examine your habits and attitude to determine your real causes of stress:

- Do you always take exhaustion as a temporary feeling ("I just have a million things in my life right now"), despite the fact that you can't recall the last time you took a break?
- Do you think of stress as a part of your job or home life ("Things are still difficult around here") or as a personality trait ("I just have a lot of nervous energy")?

STRESS MANAGEMENT TECHNIQUES

- Do you think that you are feeling stressed due to other individuals or external circumstances, or do you consider it to be completely natural and unexceptional?

- Your stress level will be out of your reach until you take the blame for your part in causing it.

Journaling: self-awareness

Do you know sometimes writing down your feelings so you can see them on paper can help you distinguish between helpful and unhelpful ideas? As you write, keep track of which ideas are logical and will help you step ahead in life versus those that are depressing and will hold you back. This will allow you to engage with constructive thinking that will assist you in solving challenges and regaining control of your life.

You should also start a stress journal to help you recognize the common stressors of your life and how you cope with them. Keep note of the depression in your journal at all times. You'll see trends and general themes when you keep a regular journal.

- What triggered the depression (make a guess if you're unsure)
- How you mentally felt.
- How you reacted to the situation.
- What you did to feel better for yourself.

STRESS MANAGEMENT TECHNIQUES

Identifying real motivations will make you more prepared and conscious the next time you come across any stressful situation.

Stress Quiz

Emotional intelligence- EI has the ability to recognize your own stress level (self-awareness). Take this quiz and score how you usually respond in any of the situations below.

- 1 = Never
- 2 = Sometimes
- 3 = Very often
- 4 = Always

You need to fill in the required number for the issue below, and add the totals and find out how stressed you are.

- Do you want to complete as much task in as little time as possible?
- Do you get irritated when you found some problems or interruptions?
- Do you always want to win all of your games in order to have fun?
- Do you ever find yourself speeding the car for beating a red light?
- Are you hesitant to ask for any assistance with a problem?
- Do you always try to get others' love and admiration?
- Do you like to criticize other people's work?

STRESS MANAGEMENT TECHNIQUES

- Do you find yourself always checking your watch or clock?
- Can you successfully manage your time?

- Do you have a habit of managing several tasks at once?
- Can you feel irritated or upset easily?

- Do you have a lot of spare time for hobbies or alone time?
- Do you have a habit of talking fast or rushing over conversations?
- Do you consider yourself to be a hard-driving individual?
- Did your friends or family members think you're a rough driver?
- Do you have a habit of working on numerous tasks at the same time?
- Do you have any deadlines?

- Do you ever feel bad for relaxing and doing nothing during your free time?
- Do you overburden yourself with responsibilities?

Total:

Results:

STRESS MANAGEMENT TECHNIQUES

If your ranking is between 20 and 30, it's quite possible that you're unproductive or that your life is uninteresting.

A ranking of 31 to 50 indicates that your ability to endure and manage stress is well balanced.

If you got a score between 51 and 60, your stress level is moderate, and you're on the verge of getting too stressed.

If the cumulative number of points reaches 60, you might be at risk for heart failure and should seek stress relief immediately.

How do you manage or cope with stress?

First of all, you need to think about how you actually deal and handle stress in your life. You should use your stress log to help you figure out what they are. Are the coping mechanisms safe or dysfunctional, productive or ineffective?

Many people, unfortunately, deal with stress in ways that worsen the problem.

Unhealthy ways of coping with stress

These coping strategies can relieve tension temporarily, but they may have harmful consequences:

STRESS MANAGEMENT TECHNIQUES

- Excessive smoking
- Excessive alcohol use
- Eating junk food or comfort foods
- Watching your favorite show on TV or monitor for long periods of time
- Excluding yourself from friends, families, and hobbies
- Using sedatives or narcotics to feel good
- Excessive sleeping
- Becoming a procrastinator
- Making the most of every minute of the day to prevent problems
- Taking your frustrations out on others (angry outbursts, physical violence)

Learning healthier ways to manage stress

It's the right time to discover healthy ways to cope with stress if your existing habits aren't helping you achieve better mental and physical health. Experiment with different methods and tactics because no one strategy fits with all. Concentrate on what makes you feel comfortable.

Let's start with 4 A's

4A's Stress relief management

You should start doing the following things to change the situation (Avoid, Alter) and change your response until you've identified the real cause of stress (Adapt, Accept). It's good to remember the four A's when determining which choice to use in any life situation:

STRESS MANAGEMENT TECHNIQUES

- Avoid or Stay away from
- Alter or Modify
- Adapt
- Accept

Avoid or eliminate

It's not a wise option to stop dealing with a difficult situation, but you might be shocked by how many stressors you can exclude from your life by avoiding negative situations when possible.

By avoiding provocations, you will give up control over stress. Stress isn't something that appears suddenly. Triggers, rather, are to blame. Working long hours, not having the equipment required for the task, and working in a stressful environment are all typical workplace triggers. You should learn to minimize the exact causes that cause the stress in your life. One of the most critical techniques to alleviate stress is to avoid it.

Controlling your environment

You know, your atmosphere indeed plays a vital role in stress, and different kinds of environments have a significant impact on your behavior and overall life satisfaction.

You just need to add something, delete something, or alter something to change the environment that surrounds you.

STRESS MANAGEMENT TECHNIQUES

For example, you can switch off the television if the news daily leaves you anxious. Taking a longer but less-traveled road if traffic makes you nervous. If walking to the grocery store seems difficult, you can shop for groceries online.

Learn the art of saying "NO"

You should respect the boundaries. Pilling up your plate more than you can eat, whether in your personal or professional life, is a sure formula for stress. Distinguish between "should" and "musts," and say "no" is important where possible.

Saying No will protect you

Saying no without feeling guilty is very important, not a selfish act. You'd actually doubt someone's senses if they asked, "Can I have the air you breathe?" You will have no guilt in saying no to them.

However, if anyone asks, "Can I ask you to do something for me that will drive you off the brink and make you feel stressed out and resentful?" you'll always agree out of habit, responsibility, or guilt. Sure, the request was certainly not expressed that way, but that is exactly what you are being asked to do.

Obviously, there are moments when we can't say no, as well as times when saying yes is in our best interests or when we just want to say yes.

STRESS MANAGEMENT TECHNIQUES

The key to avoiding discomfort and fear is to become more vigilant of our everyday lives, noticing our old knee-jerk responses. The question then becomes, is this self-awareness teaching part of your self-care routine?

All things considered and the emotions and desires of the person making the offer, the desire to say yes/okay, and most importantly, my own sanity, is it in my own interest to say yes or is it okay to refuse?" is the secret to a good self-care policy.

I believe you'll find that, as seen in this light, there are definitely a lot of situations where learning to say no is completely acceptable.

As a result, you will answer the questions, "How do I relieve fear and escape stress?" for yourself. You must learn to say no! It's all that!

Distance yourself

People who annoy you should be avoided. If a coworker makes you tensed, you can create a space between the two of you. You can attend meetings from far or stroll outside, even though it means taking a few extra steps.

Sometimes annoying people are inevitable

You need to accept this reality that irritating people do exist, and you have to communicate with them in a more respectful and acceptable manner.

STRESS MANAGEMENT TECHNIQUES

You can't always walk away from a problem, particularly if the person bothering you is a coworker or a family member. I'm not saying you should be compliant and put up with their bad behavior; instead, learn to show yourself so you can maintain your happiness and wellbeing.

Not every task on your to-do list is a must

You always need to examine your everyday activities, obligations, and timetable. If you have too many tasks on your mind, transfer non-important things to the bottom of the list or delete them altogether. In order of priority, mark the to-do list with A's, B's, and C's. Scratch the C's off your to-do page on busy days.

Make it more realistic

You're setting yourself up for frustration and stress if the list is more idealistic than what you would actually do. Second, stopping yourself from feeling accomplished by the end of the day. Plus, if you write down too many items, you're more likely to get overwhelmed. You won't know where to go, and you'll be more likely to procrastinate.

Avoid hot topics

You also need to cross religion and politics from your list of topics to discuss if they make you angry. Avoid discussion about the same question with the same people or defend yourself as it comes up in conversation.

STRESS MANAGEMENT TECHNIQUES

Altering - change your situation

Taking a record and attempting to improve the condition is one of the most beneficial things you can do when you're stressed.

Though you will not continuously be able to stop stressors, you will be able to change them. Changing a provocation to have a lower effect on your stress levels is suggested. Managing your time more effectively, for example, will reduce your stress levels. If you're feeling overworked as a result of long hours, maybe you should concentrate on time management. You will change this otherwise normal trigger so that it does not create high-stress levels by properly handling your time.

Tell them how you feel - instead of holding your emotions

Sometimes you can respectfully request other people to change their actions. If appropriate let people know how your feel. If small issues aren't addressed, they can develop into bigger ones.

Be Assertive- Communicate without any hesitation

Don't sit and watch like a spectator in your own life. Face challenges, trying the best to predict and avoid them. If a client sends you an unreasonable deadline at work, be honest with them and tell them you'll need more time to finish the job properly.

STRESS MANAGEMENT TECHNIQUES

Openly express your emotions. Have in mind to use "I'm overwhelmed by shorter deadlines and a heavier workload," for example. Is there anything we can do or a better approach we can use to get things back into balance?"

Learn the skill of Time management

Poor time management will lead to a great deal of tension. It's difficult to remain relaxed and focused when you're behind on projects. However, if you prepare accordingly and don't strain yourself, you will reduce the amount of strain you experience.

Give them a gentle reminder at first

Make it clear how much time you have at the start of a conversation by saying something like, "I'm happy to talk." Only keep in mind that I have ten minutes before I have to leave for a meeting." Alternatively, schedule your contact with other activities. When the time comes, maintain momentum and stop the conversation.

Adapting - the situation

The adaptation to stress strategy is the next move. If you can't stop or change a stressor, the only thing you can do is react to it. This will assist you with regaining control of the stressor.

STRESS MANAGEMENT TECHNIQUES

Your mental state will have a significant impact on your stress levels. Your body feels as though it is in the midst of a tense situation every time you consider a bad thought about yourself. Change your expectations and behavior about challenging circumstances to regain your energy.

Reframe your problems

Rather than thinking about your feelings of anger and helplessness, again and again, take a new look at your condition. What sides of your existing situation cause you the most anxiety? What needs aren't being fulfilled in your life?

Try to see it in a more optimistic light when you're in a difficult situation. Instead of being annoyed by a traffic jam, consider it an excuse to regroup, listen to your favorite radio station, or spend some alone time.

Draw the bigger picture

Try to consider your situation from a certain angle. Consider how critical it will be in the long term. Will that make a difference in a month? Is it only a year? Is it really worth being worked up about? If the answer is no, you should devote your time and resources to something else.

STRESS MANAGEMENT TECHNIQUES

Setting reasonable expectations

High ambitions are often a result of a need to exert control over all events and other individuals, and they can result in significant stress and mood swings.

If you redefine achievement and avoid looking for distinction, you'll feel less guilty and frustrated. Perfectionism is a big cause of depression that should be avoided. Stop expecting excellence and setting yourself up for disappointment. Establish realistic expectations for yourself and others, and learn to accept "good enough."

Attitude of gratitude

A time when you feel stressed, take a minute to think about all the things you're grateful for in your life, like your own good qualities and abilities. This direct approach will assist you with keeping things in perspective.
Gratitude gives you courage and improves your self-esteem. It is indivisibly tied to both physical and mental health. The "attitude of gratitude" is the perfect cure to tension, frustration, jealousy, and discontent because it creates satisfaction.

Allow it to become a part of your personality! Be thankful for all you have, for all the little things of your life, and also for what you don't have yet!

STRESS MANAGEMENT TECHNIQUES

Accepting- the situation

Finally, no matter how hard you try, certain circumstances obviously will not improve. Accepting this will help you with managing the stress in your life. When you try to entirely focus your time and attention on the things you can handle, you'll be much more successful. And if you can't fix any stressful scenario, it doesn't mean your feelings aren't important.

Don't try to control what's beyond your controll

Is it possible to transform a frog into a prince with a kiss? I'm hoping you said "no." Sometimes you simply can't manipulate the uncontrollable. As the great Les Brown once said "you don't know, what you don't know."

Always keep in mind that many aspects of life are beyond our understanding, especially other people's actions:

- Mindset: No matter how powerful your influence is if anyone refuses to change their perspective, try to avoid them. That's also uncontrollable. If you try to force it, you might end up stressed.
- Things happened in the past for a reason. Since you can't go back in time, leave it there. So, rather than encouraging it to annoy you, overcome it. There's nothing you can do about it.

STRESS MANAGEMENT TECHNIQUES

- You can't change people's minds: Like it or not, people make decisions.

Look always on the brighter side

"What doesn't destroy us makes us stronger," as the saying goes. When challenged by big obstacles, try to see them as tools for professional development. Try to learn from your mistakes if your bad decisions lead to a difficult situation.

Learn the art of forgiveness

Recognizing that we belong to an imperfect world where people do make mistakes.

Although forgiving power is good, it is a very difficult ability to learn. Resentment and rage will irritate you for years, keeping you trapped in the darkness of your life if you don't deal with them.

To be sure, forgiving does not imply that you should let someone who has done something wrong to you, go unaddressed. Rather, it suggests that you should unleash the toxic energy you have against them and remove those feelings from your life.

The effect of forgiveness on a person's mental and physical health is incredible. "Forgiveness has been found to ease rage, pain, and depression, and promote emotions of optimism, hope, sympathy, and self-assurance." according to the latest studies.

STRESS MANAGEMENT TECHNIQUES

Talk about your feelings

You can also have an appointment with a doctor or talk to a good friend personally. And if there's nothing you can do to change the stressful situation, just sharing what you're going through can be really helpful. It is not a sign of failure to open up, and it would not make you a burden to anyone. In reality, most friends will be pleased that you have enough faith in them to reveal your feelings to them, and this will only deepen your friendship.

Chapter 3:
Coping with Stress with Physical Fitness

PHYSICAL FITNESS

Do you know that some physical exercise can help you reduce your overall stress levels and strengthen your mental and physical well-being? Let's find out more about it.

How does your brain respond?

Physical exercise increases your blood supply and improves the body's capacity to use oxygen. Both of these changes will have an immediate impact on your brain. Exercise also boosts endorphin activity in the brain. Endorphins are the "feel-good" neurotransmitters responsible for the well-known "runner's high." This is the feeling of happiness and joy that many people experience after exercising.

Physical exercise will also assist in diverting your attention away from your problems. Exercise encourages you to concentrate on your body rather than your thoughts because it involves regular movements. When exercising, focusing on the pace of the activities has much of the same effects as meditation.

Regular exercise has been proven to:

- Decrease stress
- Improve your mood
- Stop anxiety
- Increase your self-confidence
- Improve your sleeping habits

PHYSICAL FITNESS

Exercise also has these added health benefits:

Exercise is helpful and can strengthen your spirit, increases your stamina, and lower your blood pressure.

- It builds up and tones muscles.
- It helps to develop your bones.
- It helps in the reduction of body fat.
- It gives you a toned and stable body.

According to one scientific study, regular aerobic activity has been shown to reduce general levels of tension, elevate and regulate mood, increase sleep, and improve self-esteem. Even five minutes of aerobic activity will help to reduce anxiety. Before getting started, let's cover some basic questions.

How to choose what exercise is best for me?

Here are some important things to think about before starting an exercise routine for managing your stress:

- What kinds of physical workouts do I love doing?
- Do I prefer to participate in group activities?
- What classes are the most suitable for my schedule?
- Do I have any physical problems that can restrict my workout options?

PHYSICAL FITNESS

- What specific objectives do I have in mind? (For example, weight loss, muscle strengthening, endurance improvement, or mood enhancement.

Tips to get started

You should make an easy-to-follow exercise schedule when you first start your workout program. When you've gotten used to your schedule, you might start changing up your workout hours and tasks.
Here we compile some important tips to help you before start:

- Always select an exercise that you love. Exercising can be very pleasurable.
- Make your workout routine a part of your daily routine. Put it on your schedule if you need reminders.
- Variety is important in life. Make sure your workouts are different, so you don't get bored. Find a variety of fitness classes at the nearest gym or community center.
- Don't overspend on fitness plans. Avoid purchasing fitness club memberships or costly machines unless you want to use them on a daily basis.
- Don't quit. Exercise can become part of your life. Create a habit and do so on a daily basis, and it will help in the reduction of sadness or stress.

PHYSICAL FITNESS

Types of physical activities that help in stress relief

You can add solo exercises like cycling, hiking, Mindfulness, or yoga and mix with social activities like high-intensity interval fitness classes or occasional group walks or bike rides in your workout routine.

Yoga

Yoga is a holistic wellness and spiritual growth system that incorporates breathing exercises, and physical postures. Yoga doesn't have much of a cardiovascular benefit unless you're performing an active flow in a yoga session. However, it will help you how to unwind, relieve tension, stretch tight muscles, and even reinforce weak ones.

Yoga can help to reduce discomfort and increase feelings of wellbeing when practiced on a daily basis. According to a 2016 study of the use of yoga for anxiety and depression, exercise can help with anxiety, depression, and symptoms of post-traumatic stress disorder (PTSD).

Mindfulness meditation

In recent years, mindfulness has gained a lot of attention from actors, corporate owners, and psychologists. So, what does mindfulness involve? Rather than imagining the future or remembering the past, mindfulness directs your attention to the current moment in your life, allowing you to be completely immersed in it.

PHYSICAL FITNESS

A basic mindfulness meditation:

- First step: you will need to find a peaceful place where you won't be disturbed or distracted by anybody.
- Sit in a chair; you must feel comfortable with your back straight.
- Close your eyes and concentrate on one thing, such as your breathing and the sound of air rushing into and out of your nostrils, or the raising and lowering of your belly or a symbolic expression that you repeat in the meditation.
- When you first start your training, you will notice that your thoughts keep returning in the form of your fears or regrets. But don't be discouraged. Each time when you bring your focus back to the moment, you're building a new habit that will help you in focusing on the present or help you stop worrying about the past or about the future. Using an app or audio download to center your attention may also be helpful, particularly when you're first starting out.

Don't be concerned with the distracting feelings in your mind or how good you're doing. If thoughts interrupt your relaxing session, don't fight with them; instead, softly and without judgment, return your mind to your focus.

Breathing Exercise to Try

You will note that your heart rate and breathing rate increase when you feel nervous.

PHYSICAL FITNESS

You may start to sweat and feel dizzy or lightheaded as well. When you're feeling nervous, controlling your breathing will help you calm both your body and mind.

Here's how to get started in less than five minutes. If you can, try it right now.

- To start, take a comfortable position by sitting on a chair. Your back must be straight and your feet on the ground; place your hands on your lap. Instead, you can also lay down on a sofa or on a rug. If you want to, close your eyes.

- Pay attention to your emotions. Are you feeling good or tense? Is your mind cool or circling with ideas? Is your breathing deep and steady or shallow and fast? Are the muscles relaxed, or are they tense?

- To the count of 1...2...3, gently and thoroughly inhale through your nose.

- Gently exhale from the mouth to the count of 1...2...3...4.

- Do this four times at least.

- As you breathe in, feel the tension in your body and mind slowly disperse, and as you breathe out, feel the tightness disperse.

PHYSICAL FITNESS

Reconnect with yourself after completing this breathing exercise. Is there a difference between how the mind and body feel? Do you feel any difference?

Visualizing

Have you ever used the phrase "looking for your happy place"? Painting an image in mind of a relaxing location will potentially help to stimulate your mind and body.

For this exercise, you will have to sit in a calm and relaxed spot when you start to feel nervous. Consider where you'd like to relax. Although it can be any location on the planet, actual or imagined, it should be a picture that makes you feel relaxed, content, quiet, and safe. Consider how many little things you'd notice if you were there. Consider how the whole setting will smell, feel, and sound. Imagine yourself in that place, relaxing and enjoying it.

After some time, open your eyes and take long, steady breaths through your nose and out of your mouth until you have a clear view of your "happy spot." Try to concentrate on the spot you've planned in your mind and be conscious of your breathing before you see your fear dissipate. When you're feeling nervous, go to this location in your mind.

PHYSICAL FITNESS

Progressive muscle relaxation

Progressive muscle relaxation is a two-step procedure that involves carefully stressed and relaxing various muscle groups in the body. It gives you an instinctual experience with how tension—as well as total relaxation—feels in various areas of the body with daily practice. This will assist you in reacting to the first symptoms of stress-related muscle tension. Your mind will relax as your body does.

For added stress relief, progressive muscle relaxing may be paired with deep breathing.

Practicing progressive muscle relaxation

- If you previously deal with back pain, muscle contractions, or other medical problems that may be aggravated by tensing muscles, you need to talk to your doctor first.
- First of all, start at your feet and work your way up to your face, concentrating on just tensing the muscles that are supposed to be tense.
- Take off your shoes, loosen your clothing, and feel comfortable.
- For 2 to 3 minutes, breathe slowly and deeply in and out.
- When you're ready, concentrate on your right foot. Take a few moments to notice how it looks.

PHYSICAL FITNESS

Tai Chi

Tai Chi is a traditional Chinese exercise that is performed all over the world. It has been found to improve immune function as well as increase blood levels of feel-good endorphins, making it valuable to those who suffer from anxiety and depression.

Tai Chi is easy to understand and practice because the movements are simple and regular. It does not necessitate stamina or agility but rather stresses movement type and breathing. Tai Chi is regarded as a self-healing exercise. The procedure, according to traditional Chinese medicine, aids in the alleviation of energy blockages in the body and aids in the prevention or treatment of certain diseases.

Tai Chi has been shown to improve general wellbeing and helpful in controlling different issues, including depression, anxiety, tension, and mood disturbances, as well as self-esteem.

Gardening

Working in the garden will help you in feeling good. Stretching, bending, cutting, and moving seeds, compost, or watering around the garden can help you beautify your place and relax your mind while working a variety of muscles and elevating your heart rate marginally.

PHYSICAL FITNESS

Aerobic exercises that can curb stress and anxiety

Jogging

If your knees allow it, consider jogging or biking for still more anxiety relief. Only make sure you're on the safe side of the road and wearing shoes that have good protection and cushioning.

Brisk walk

Going on a brisk walk is another easy way to do some stress-relieving exercise. According to the Anxiety and Depression Association of America, results show that a 10-minute stroll can help maintain balance and can be almost as effective as a 45-minute or longer walk in alleviating tension and anxiety.

Cycling

Cycling is an easy and good cardiovascular exercise. You only need to wear a helmet and a comfortable outfit. Keep an eye out for traffic and potholes. Alternatively, for the safest experience, get on a stationary cycle.

Swimming

Swimming is a kind of full-body exercise and also has some strength training features because water is denser than air and can resist your movements rather than when you walk on the ground.

PHYSICAL FITNESS

For some people, being immersed in water is also really relaxing and can help them relax even more.

Boxing

Do you ever try to hit something when you're stressed or angry? If you have a punching bag, boxing can be a great way to relieve tension, rage, and other negative feelings while still getting a great heart-pumping exercise.

Dancing

Is there anything more uplifting or enjoyable than dancing to some fine music? Dancing is an excellent way to relieve tension while still enjoying a good workout. It can also be a really social experience, which can make you feel more connected and supported, which can help you feel less stressed.

Music

"Music listening seems to be able to change brain activity to the same level as medicine," according to Stanford University researchers. They pointed out that music can be enjoyed by anyone, making it a simple stress-reduction tool.

Music has some sort of unseen power that has an impact on both the mind and the body. Faster music will help you relax, and you will feel more energetic. Music can increase your mood and make you feel more assertive about life.

PHYSICAL FITNESS

A slow pace will calm your mind and loosen your muscles, helping you feel calmer and letting go of the day's tension. Music will help you relax and control your stress.

High-intensity interval training- HIIT

High-intensity interval training (HIIT) exercise gets the heart pumping quickly by combining aerobic, anaerobic, and resistance components into a short exercise that can pay major health and fitness dividends.

Bedtime Routine for better sleep

Many people with stress problems have difficulty sleeping, and it can be difficult to determine whether you can't sleep because you're stressed or you can't sleep because you're not feeling sleepy. It's possible that the answer is both. The truth is that tension and anxiety can trigger or worsen sleeping problems. Sleep deprivation has an effect on the mood, which can lead to irritability and depression. During various stages of sleep, vital brain processes occur that leave you feeling refreshed and energized while still assisting you in learning and memory building.

If the relaxing methods mentioned above can be integrated into your nighttime routine, you can do some other activities.

PHYSICAL FITNESS

A bedtime routine is a series of tasks you do in the 30 to 60 minutes before bedtime in the same order every night. Bedtime rituals differ, but they often involve relaxing practices such as taking a warm bath, reading, journaling, or meditation.

Some tips to consider before going to bed:

- Avoid caffeine: 6 hours before bedtime, caffeine will affect your sleep.
- Avoid energetic exercise: While daily exercise can help you sleep better, you can save your strenuous exercises for the morning or afternoon.
- Music: When you get ready for bed, listen to a piece of calming music to help release hormones that increase your mood. Feeling physically at ease will also make the body relax.
- Provide a comfortable sleeping atmosphere. Examine the sleeping condition for potential stressors. A healthy sleeping condition is dim and quiet.
- Take a heated bath or shower. This will not only help you calm and de-stress, but it will also lower your body temperature, which will be beneficial to your health.

When your tired, these home remedies will also help you sleep better. If sleep continues to elude you, seek medical advice. There might be other, more serious, underlying sleep conditions.

Chapter 4:

Ways to Manage Stress with Nutrition

MANAGE STRESS WITH NUTRITION

Though short-term stress can cause headaches, stomach cramps, weight gain, and more cold and flu episodes, constant stress affects every part of your body, including your digestive and reproductive systems as well as your immune system. According to the National Institute of Mental Health, if it is left untreated, constant stress will increase the chance of type 2 diabetics, obesity, cardiac disease, depression, and anxiety (NIMH).

That's right: Stress can not only make you irritable, but it can also make you fat and ill.

How stress affects our appetite?

Stress can affect appetite

Stress can suppress appetite for a short time. The hypothalamus, a brain organ, produces a corticotrophin-releasing hormone, which suppresses appetite. The hippocampus also sends signals to the adrenal glands, which are located on top of the kidneys, to release the hormone epinephrine (also known as adrenaline). Epinephrine aids in the activation of the body's fight-or-flight reflex; it is a physical condition that can stop feeding.

It's a different matter whether stress lasts or is continues. Cortisol, an important hormone created by the adrenal glands, increases appetite and can also increase motivation in general, including the desire to feed.

MANAGE STRESS WITH NUTRITION

Cortisol levels can drop after a traumatic episode, but if the tension doesn't go away — or if a person's stress response is trapped in the "on" spot — cortisol levels may remain high.

Stress leads to overeating

Binge eating disorder and the urge to overeat can also be caused by stress. Food is also used by people with the condition to cope with tension and other feelings they want to suppress, such as anger, depression, and boredom.

It can start out a binge-eating circle that goes something like this:

- When you're nervous, you eat a lot.
- You feel guilty or concerned about gaining weight after overeating, which leaves you much more depressed.

Increased appetite after a stressful period

The human body, sometimes, can go into a "recovery mode" after a difficult time, resulting in increased appetite and food cravings. Simultaneously, metabolic rates decrease to conserve energy.

Being mindful of these habits can help you control your stress levels, and you can help your body heal from difficult times more quickly and reduce harmful effects, including weight gain, by improving your nutrition and diet.

MANAGE STRESS WITH NUTRITION

Balanced and healthy diet is a key

Eating a nutritious and healthy diet is very important for our bodies and helps us to deal with those changes that are brought about by stress.

Foods and drinks you should include

But don't worry; there are various foods that you can incorporate into your diet to improve digestive health and potentially alleviate stress levels. Here are some of them:

Fatty Fish

Fatty fish is found to be high in omega-3 fatty acids, including alpha-linolenic acid, which can help in stress and anxiety relief. Salmon, mackerel, and trout should be included in your diet.

Eggs

Minerals, amino acids, vitamins, and protein abound in whole eggs, making them a nutritional powerhouse. They're also high in choline, a nutrient that's vital for brain health and can help you avoid stress.

Parsley

This healthy herb comprises free radicals that guard against oxidative stress, which is linked to a variety of illnesses, including depression and anxiety.

MANAGE STRESS WITH NUTRITION

It also includes carotenoids, flavonoids, and volatile oils, both of which are potent antioxidants that aid in inflammation reduction.

Garlic

Stress will drain your energy and have a significant effect on your immune system. Garlic is an antioxidant-rich food that helps to reduce stress by defusing free radicals in the body.

Colorful fruit and vegetables

You need to try different fruit or vegetables together for eating. Antioxidants used in fruits and vegetables tend to suppress inflammation.

Look for: those with a bright red, as the darker the color, the healthier they are.

Dark Chocolate

After all, those stress-induced chocolate cravings might be necessary. Dark chocolate is an excellent stress reliever to use in your diet. According to studies, eating dark chocolate will help people who are depressed lower their stress hormone levels.

Live foods

Eating some fermented foods can aid in gut health, according to research. Live yogurts, sauerkraut and kimchi, miso soups, and dark chocolate are also good options.

MANAGE STRESS WITH NUTRITION

Turmeric

Turmeric includes curcumin, a bioactive agent that reduces inflammation and oxidative stress, which can help reduce anxiety. It increases serotonin and dopamine levels, which can help people who feel anxious or depressed.

Whole Grains

Eating nutritious carbs, according to studies, will increase serotonin levels, a hormone that improves mood and decreases tension. Sweet potatoes and whole grains, for example, can help with this. However, you can consume only good, unrefined carbohydrates.

Avocados

Avocados are high in omega-3 fatty acids, phytochemicals, fiber, and other important nutrients that can aid with stress relief, concentration, and mood enhancement. Avocados, according to a report published in the Nutrition Journal, will increase food quality and reduce the risk of metabolic syndrome, a category of disorders that includes elevated blood pressure and obesity.

Nuts

Nuts almonds, pistachios, and walnuts contain many important nutrients, such as B vitamins, magnesium, vitamin E, and zinc, and help the body control stress levels and improve the immune system.

MANAGE STRESS WITH NUTRITION

Black Tea

Drinking black tea will make you heal faster from difficult situations. People who drank 4 cups of tea every day for 6 weeks were compared to people who drank another liquid. After difficult situations, tea drinkers indicated feeling calmer and having lower levels of the stress hormone cortisol.

Water

Do you know drinking more water plays an important role in relieving tension? Dehydration can cause stress because our bodies need water to work properly.

Milk

Do you know that having a glass of milk before bed or at some other time of the day can help you to feel relax? Lactium, a protein found in milk, makes the body calm by reducing blood pressure and potassium, which helps muscles relax.

Fruit Juice

Vitamin C-rich juices, such as orange juice, grapefruit juice, and strawberry juice, may help relieve stress levels by reducing cortisol levels in the body.

MANAGE STRESS WITH NUTRITION

Green Tea

If you're a coffee addict, you might not be aware of the negative impact caffeine has on your body. If you steadily wean yourself off of high doses of caffeine, you will reduce your stress levels and increase your mental productivity during the day. Replacing coffee with decaffeinated green tea, which has a calming flavor and plenty of antioxidants, is a surprisingly easy and safe way.

Foods and drinks you should avoid

Here are some foods and drinks that you should avoid.

Salt

Salt is one way to spice food. However, sprinkling so much salt on your food can cause your body to retain sodium, which can lead to fluid accumulation, high blood pressure, and hypertension. Your heart is put under more strain as a result of this. You need to take less than 2,300 mg of salt a day to keep the sodium and stress levels down.

Sugary foods

A refined food that has more than 5 g of sugar per 100 g is considered to have a medium amount of sugar and should be avoided. Snack bars, cereals, cakes and cookies, fizzy drinks, and fruity yogurts should be avoided.

MANAGE STRESS WITH NUTRITION

Foods high in saturated fat

In periods of discomfort, all packaged food containing more than 1.5 g of saturated fat per 100 g should be avoided. Pizza, ready meals, crisps, snack bars, and pastry are only a few examples.

White carbs

You need to avoid eating white bread, rice, and noodles. Our gut bacteria enjoy whole grain goodness. Instead, use brown wholegrain alternates.

Caffeinated drinks

Moreover, caffeinated beverages can make some people feel more stressed. If you're feeling depressed, consider switching to decaffeinated drinks for a week or two to find out if it makes any difference in your life.

Alcohol

It is true that we drink alcohol to de-stress after a stressful day: it's technically a depressant, which means it serves as a slight sedative, briefly calming us down. However, if we drink too much, alcohol will deepen distress in people who already have it. Worse, since alcohol is a depressant, it will lower our levels of serotonin, the hormone linked to happiness, leading to a rise in stress and depression.

MANAGE STRESS WITH NUTRITION

Normal drinking is described by the Centers for Disease Control and Prevention as one drink a day for women and less than three drinks per day for men.

Tips for a healthy and balanced diet in your daily routine

Here are some tips for leading a stress-free life.

Never skip breakfast

You should not skip your breakfast if you don't feel hungry or think you don't have enough time. Breakfast serves to kick-start your journey for the day and also helps to regulate your blood sugar levels, reducing stress. To reap the advantages, combine berries or fruit juice with a wholegrain cereal.

Eat regularly throughout the day

Your goal is to make sure to have at least five servings of fruit and vegetables per day, with more focus on foods rich in Vitamins B and C, as well as Magnesium.

To sustain blood sugar levels, we must feed consistently during the day and not miss any meals, but we should also ensure that we are not feeling hungry. It would be much more daunting if we are anxious and have a strong desire for something while still being hungry. The first move is to make sure you're not missing any meals.

MANAGE STRESS WITH NUTRITION

Find alternatives

It's pointless to decide to replace your favorite snack with the one you don't like since this would do nothing to improve your mood. Instead, find something you enjoy eating that your body enjoys as well.

If you like jelly cookies, for example, consider substituting a little handful of dried fruit.

Pay attention

You need to keep track of how you feel when you eat and drink. If you suffer from anxiety or depression, keeping a diet and food diary can be helpful. That way, at the end of the week, you'll be able to look back to see if there are any trigger foods impacting your mood.

Avoid Emotional eating

When you're tired, try to avoid eating food. When you're struggling to ingest your meal, stress diverts blood supply away from your digestive tract, which you don't like. Bloating, gas and nausea are also possible side effects.

Practice mindful eating

Mindful eating entails having a satisfying relationship with food; it is not a strict diet; rather, it entails focusing on the enjoyment of food and being entirely aware during the meal.

MANAGE STRESS WITH NUTRITION

In comparison to mindless feeding, which can lead to people eating a lot of food but not feeling whole, mindful eating promotes a neurological warning to overeating by paying attention to body cues like thirst, fullness, and pleasure.

Experts recommend beginning with mindful eating in small steps, such as eating one meal a day or week in a slower, more careful way. Here are some pointers (and tricks) to get you started:

- You can set your kitchen timer for 20 minutes and eat a normal meal during that period.
- When lifting food, use your non-dominant side; if you're a righty, use your left hand to hold your fork.
- If you're not used to using chopsticks, give them a try.
- For five minutes, eat quietly, thinking about everything that went into making the food or different factors that play an important role from the sun's rays to the farmer to the grocer to the cook.
- Take little bites and chew them carefully.
- It is also very important to think, "Am I really hungry?" before opening the fridge or drawer every time. You can take a break or can do something else, like reading or taking a quick stroll to divert your attention.

MANAGE STRESS WITH NUTRITION

Vitamin and Mineral Supplements

All supplements appear to aid in stress management. However, the evidence for these supplements is small, and much further research is needed. Before consuming some vitamin or mineral supplements, consult with your doctor.

Key nutrients to focus

Here are some important food nutrients:

Vitamin C

Vitamin C can be obtained from a wide variety of fresh fruits and vegetables. It is stored in the adrenal gland, which is essential for the production of cortisol.

Magnesium

Magnesium levels drop sharply at times of stress, and deficiency symptoms include nausea, anxiety, insomnia, and a proclivity to stress. To get enough magnesium, eat a lot of dark green leafy vegetables, whole grains, nuts, and seeds.

Vitamins B

B vitamins, especially B5, can help to promote adrenal function by directly supporting the adrenal cortex and hormone development. Nuts, whole grains, and seeds are also good sources.

MANAGE STRESS WITH NUTRITION

Finally!

Eating a well-balanced and healthy diet can make you feel healthier. It can also aid in mood regulation. For energy, your meals should include plenty of vegetables, berries, whole grains, and lean protein. Try to have this things on a consistent basis. It's bad for you and can put you in a bad mood, which can make you more stressed.

Chapter 5:

Expert Stress Management Strategies

STRESS MANAGEMENT STRATEGIES

Job stress is described by the National Institute for Occupational Safety and Health in the United States as unhealthy physical and emotional reactions that arise when job conditions do not meet the worker's skills, resources, or needs. Workplace stress will result in poor health and, in some cases, even cause injuries.

Many employees experience stress at work, which has a negative impact on their success and well-being. According to a new survey by Northwestern National Life, about 40% of people said their jobs were incredibly stressful. Another Yale University study found that 29% of staff experience severe stress as a result of their careers.

Some general causes of stress in the workplace include:

- People feel rushed, under demand, and tired due to the extra load of work and unreasonable deadlines.

- Extra workloads give people the impression that their talents are underutilized. It has the potential to make people feel insecure about their employment.

- Lack of power - not being able to complete difficult job tasks.

- Job insecurity- employees experience extreme tension as a result of their fear of losing their jobs and having to meet high work demands.

STRESS MANAGEMENT STRATEGIES

- Anyone was feeling lonely due to a lack of emotional support or bad working relationships.

- If an employee's skill set does not meet the position requirements, he is working on a task that he is not qualified for. Then there would be stress as a result of the requests, which include strict deadlines to poor job performance.

- Adapting to change - Difficulty settling into a new job place, both in terms of meeting the expectations of the new job and adapting to future shifts in social relationships.

- Abuse or bullying.

- The blame game, in which people feel fearful for committing mistakes or admitting to them.

- There is no incentive or acknowledgment for appreciating an employee's contribution, which causes depression and jeopardizes potential attempts.

- Poor management - this gives workers the impression that they don't have the right sense of direction.

- Extreme supervision - this will make workers feel unappreciated and lower their self-esteem.

STRESS MANAGEMENT STRATEGIES

- Several reporting lines - unclear command structures, with each boss requesting that their work should be prioritized.

- Poor contact - Failure to keep staff updated of new market shifts, leading them to be concerned about their career prospects.

- Inadequate physical working conditions, such as unnecessary heat, cold, or noise, inadequate ventilation, cramped seating, defective facilities, and so on.

- Workplace conflict is another common source of stress.

The office, as you can see, is a major cause of stress. It depends on us how we recognize our stressors and develop effective coping mechanisms to improve them.

How work stress affect the employee?

Some of the most important and clear stress effects are linked to a person's ability to do his work, think clearly, and concentrate for long periods of time.

- Difficulty in focusing
- Exhaustion
- Sleep problems
- Migraines
- Feeling dizzy
- Decision-making difficulties
- Always feeling concerned

STRESS MANAGEMENT STRATEGIES

- Anxiety
- Insecurities about life and relations

Someone who is stressed can become so mentally exhausted that they are unable to do their job effectively, or if they do, the daily stresses of their job may cause their mental health to worsen even further.
Employers should offer support and understanding to their stressed employees because they might be worried due to their personal weakness.

How to decrease the effects of workplace stress?

There are quick, realistic steps you should take to restore your strength when job and career stress threaten you.

Time Management skills:

Establish a balance between work and family life

To control stress, it is very important to find a balance between work and family life. You should make an effort to strike a balance between work and family life, social gatherings and your life interests, everyday commitments, and relaxation activities.

Leave earlier for a job in the morning.

Also, 10-15 minutes will be the difference between speeding through your day and taking your time. Set your clocks and watch early if you're still late to have more time for yourself and reduce your stress levels.

STRESS MANAGEMENT STRATEGIES

Regular short breaks is a must-do thing

You need to take small breaks in the day to go for a stroll, talk to someone like your friend, or perform a relaxing technique. For lunch, try to get away from your desk or workstation. It will help you in relaxing and recharging, allowing you to be more involved rather than less.

Distinguish between the "should" and the "musts."

Avoid arranging activities back-to-back or having stuff excessively into one day to avoid overcommitting yourself. If you have to do many tasks at the same time, separate the "should" from the "musts." Tasks that aren't absolutely important should be moved to the bottom of the list or eliminated.

Draw healthy lines

Many people believe that they must be available 24 hours a day or that they should always search their smartphones for work-related notifications. However, it's important to schedule time. This may include not monitoring emails or taking job calls at home on weekends or evenings.
Handling task

Deal with the high-priority tasks first

If you have an important and tough task to perform, complete it as soon as possible. As a result, the rest of the day will be more enjoyable.

STRESS MANAGEMENT STRATEGIES

Break the complex or large projects into smaller units

If a large project feels daunting, break it down into small steps rather than doing it all at once.

Learn the art of being able to Delegate

You don't have to do everything alone. You need to allow yourself to let go of the need to be in control of every single move. In the meantime, you'll be releasing undue tension.

Don't make yourself rigid

You must be able to make compromises. If you and your manager can change your standards a bit, you may be able to reach a comfortable middle ground that lowers everyone's stress levels.

Perfectionism

You should set yourself up for failure when you set ambitious expectations for yourself. No one would expect you to do something better. Perfectionism creates stress, so avoid it.

Humor, use it appropriately

Do you know laughter can be an effective stress reliever in the workplace? Find a way to lighten the mood by telling a joke or an amusing story while you or anyone around you are taking work too seriously.

STRESS MANAGEMENT STRATEGIES

Make the working environment workable

If your desk or workroom looks like a mess, get rid of the junk; just knowing where it is will save time and reduce tension.

Complete break from work

If you think you're not doing well, take a full break from work. You can use leaves reserve for your sick days, do whatever you can to get out of the problem. Take advantage of the time out to re-energize and gain perspective.

Talk to your employer

Employees that perform well and remain happy are more productive, meaning the boss has an opportunity to reduce job tension as much as possible. Rather than involving in any quarrel, tell your boss the particular circumstances that are affecting your job results.

Find your purpose and joy in a job

Boredom or dissatisfaction with how you spend your workday will lead to high levels of stress and can have a very serious impact on your health. For all of us, though, finding a dream career that is meaningful and fulfilling is just that: a fantasy. And if you aren't in a position to search for another work that you like and are passionate about—and most of us aren't— you can always find meaning and fulfillment in a profession that you don't like.

STRESS MANAGEMENT STRATEGIES

Rotating shifts

Working late at night, or waking up early in the morning, or changing your shifts can affect your sleep quality, which can affect your health and can result in making you more stressed.

- To avoid sleep loss, try to limit the odd shifts you work in a series.
- If you want to keep the sleep routine consistent, avoid changing shifts.

Other tips to reduce the workload

We already talked about these points in detail.

- Make smart diet decisions
- Adopt a healthier lifestyle and workout on a regular basis
- Make sleeping a habit
- Make use of 4 as strategies.
- Avoid Negative thoughts
- Discuss with friends

Chapter 6: Benefits of Dealing with Stress

BENEFITS OF DEALING WITH STRESS

Have you ever wondered what good stress is? It's not as bad for your health as you would imagine. If you like horror movies, you know how it feels when the murderer is lurking around the corner, the last hero alive is hidden behind a tree, and your pulse is racing. Yes, you're under a lot of tension about what will happen next. You're still enthralled, fascinated, and curious to see what happens next.

Stress isn't really a bad thing. In reality, a small amount may be useful. The kind of stress you get when you're nervous about something, like a first date or overcoming a job problem, is referred to as "eustress" by psychologists.

Characteristics of eustress

Eustress, or positive stress, has the following characteristics:

- It motivates and increases your energy.
- It is thought to be under your coping capabilities.
- You feel enthralled.
- It enhances efficiency.
- Eustress drives you to higher levels of efficiency. It motivates you to do new things in your job, finish that rough exercise, and tackle that big renovation project.
- Stress, even in minimal or moderate form, will make you feel better, wiser, and healthier.

BENEFITS OF DEALING WITH STRESS

Positive side of stress

Now is the time to learn about the unexpected ways stress can be beneficial to your health (yes, really!).

Stress may improve your immune system

Though long-term, continuous stress can make you more susceptible to sickness, short-term "good" stress can help you from becoming sick. Eustress boosts the immune system's efficacy. Manageable levels of stress, according to research, can promote tolerance and disease resistance, according to a review of studies published in Psychoneuroendocrinology in 2013.

It keeps you motivated

"Exactly what you need to get the job done at work." Consider a deadline: it's right in front of you, and it's going to motivate you to handle the situation more efficiently, quickly, and productively. The trick is to see challenging conditions as an obstacle rather than a daunting, impossible roadblock.

Eustress may also assist you in entering a state of "flow," which is characterized by heightened concentration and full immersion in a task.

Flow can occur in the workplace (such as playing a musical instrument), and it is primarily fueled by the desire to do your best.

BENEFITS OF DEALING WITH STRESS

Stress can make you tough

There's no doubt that overcoming difficulty creates resiliency. When you first encounter something, you can believe it is the worst situation ever because you don't know how to deal with it. However, as you face new circumstances and tackle new challenges, you are preparing yourself to cope with additional situations in the future.

For example, consider a difficult situation you've had in the past. When it first happened, how did you deal with the stress? Let's jump forward to the moment. Have you recently dealt with a similar situation? If that's the case, how did you approach the issue the second time? Almost certainly, you did. You actually feel more in control because you knew what to expect and what the consequences were. As a result, you didn't give in or crumble under pressure. This is how you become stronger as a result of the tension.

Stress gives you self-confidence

Stress will help you increasing self-trust. If you've mastered working in tense scenarios, you'll have the guarantee that regardless of what happens, you'll be able to handle everything.
Stress can be a huge source of disruption in your life, or you can learn to cope with it in a manner that benefits you, makes you emotionally healthier, and prepares you to tackle whatever life throws at you.

BENEFITS OF DEALING WITH STRESS

Enhance child development

Pregnant women often fear that their own stress will harm their unborn children—and it will if it's serious. However, according to a 2006 Johns Hopkins study, most children of mothers who registered mild to moderate stress levels during pregnancy had a better motor and developmental abilities by the age of two than children of mothers who were not stressed.

Lastly

A life free of stress isn't always possible. Consider the situation of a graduate student. The selection process is competitive, the coursework can be difficult, and transitioning from an undergraduate to a business environment can be a learning process after graduation. However, in the end, one should be proud of what one has done. The things we should be proud of and that give meaning to our lives are difficult; removing stress will certainly remove much of the meaning of our lives. It is entirely up to you how you see the stressors.

In 2013 Dr. Kelly McGonigal gave a very popular TedTalk that as of this date, has over 11 million views on YouTube. In the end she has the statistical data to back up the reality that you control how much stress effects you, and it is literally a matter of your life or your death.

The beautiful of that reality is that you do have a choice. You can be a victim, or you can be victorious!

Conclusion

CONCLUSION

Stress is something that we all know, experience, and have had to put up with it daily. Our daily lives are moving at a quick pace, and the world in which we live is becoming more complicated. Our culture, without a doubt, has an effect on all fields and professional life. Learning to better reduce stress at work or home is important for good health.

Identifying the real cause behind stress in your life is the first step in stress control. This isn't as easy as it seems. We often ignore our own stress-inducing emotions and habits because we have no idea about the real reason behind it. You may be aware that you are increasingly concerned with your job burden. However, it's possible that deadline tension is caused by your own mistake rather than the real work demands.

Pressure and problems at work, as well as an individual's lifestyle, can create stress. If you're feeling depressed for a longer time than normal, or if it's interfering with your home or work life, you need to take it seriously. Therapy, medicine, and other methods can be helpful. Meanwhile, there are techniques for dealing with stress that you should follow in order to control it.

You must find a system of self-care that works for you. For example, some people find various social behaviors useful, such as keeping a healthier lifestyle by eating well, having adequate sleep and exercise, and avoiding alcohol and drugs.

CONCLUSION

You must focus on stress management by learning to think differently. Understanding when to let go of a situation and speaking positively about your life will help you from getting depressed over small issues. Controlling your thoughts is just half the battle; once you focus on reducing stress by a healthier lifestyle and dietary modifications, you will stop worsening anxiety problems.

In this book, you will read about several stress strategies that will help you in making your plan for changing your life. A complete diet information to control stress is added in this book. You may be surprised, but it's true that not every stress is harmful to your health. This book covers some of the amazing benefits of stress, and how you can use it to your advantage!

Keep in mind that only you, not the outside world, will determine if you are going to live a stress-free life or not. You can reduce stress. Even use it to your advantage, and live a longer, healthy and more productive life!

Proverbs 18:21 King James Bible

Death and life are in the power of the tongue: and they that love it shall eat the fruit thereof.

The Stress Management Book
Expert Habits for Dealing With Stress for Men, Women, Teens & Kids

We want to thank you for the purchase of this book and more importantly, thank you for reading it to the end. We hope your reading experience was pleasurable and that you would inform your family and friends on Facebook, Twitter or other social media.

We would like to continue to provide you with high-quality books, and that end, would you mind leaving us a review on Amazon.com?

Just use the link below, scroll down about 3/4 of the page and you will see images similar to the one below.

We are extremely grateful for your assistance.
Warm Regards, MahoneyProducts Publishing

HERE IS THE REVIEW LINK:
https://www.amazon.com/dp/B09419FG8H

You might also enjoy:

THE BOOK ON PUBERTY FOR GIRLS

Growing up can present young girls with many challenges. These challenges are much easier to overcome when the young girls have understanding about their bodies changes, and the knowledge and comfort of knowning they are all a natural part of life.

This book covers the basics first, like what Puberty is and the expected growth during that time. Then we'll examine some details of the way a girl's body tends to develop. We will start small, noting the first changes in height, weight, and hair growth, and then we'll work toward the more essential changes like breast development, diet and exercise, and menstruation. All in easy to understand language.

Discover...

* Puberty for Girls: Complete Overview

* Breast Development and Bras

* Menstrual Cycle: Your Period

* Fitness Food and Nutrition

* Precocious Puberty

* Solutions to Puberty and Emotions

* Expert tips to teach Parents how to navigate this special time in their child's life.

Each section written with easy to understand language and covers every detail needed to navigate every challenge.

So get excited! Feel comfortable with the knowledge and understanding your young princess is about to discover on this amazing life journey!

Amazon.com Book Link:

https://www.amazon.com/dp/B092467B4B

www.ingramcontent.com/pod-product-compliance
Lightning Source LLC
Chambersburg PA
CBHW060252030426
42335CB00014B/1660